HOW TO BE HAPPY
ON YOUR OWN

HAPPY WHO?
HAPPY YOU!

Learn How To Live Life On
Your Own Terms

Carter Roberts

Table of Contents

PART 1 5
Chapter 1: Happy People Stay Present 6
Chapter 2: Don't Wait Another Second To Live Your Dreams 10
Chapter 3: Why You Need To Find Your Why 13
Chapter 4: Why Helping Others Can Make You Happier 16
Chapter 5: How to Reprogram Your Mind for Success 18
Chapter 6: *The Downside of Work-Life Balance* 22
Chapter 7: How to Eat With Mood in Mind 25
Chapter 8: Playing To Your Strengths 28
Chapter 9: Overcoming Fear and Self-Doubt 32
Chapter 10: How to Share Your Talent 35
PART 2 38
Chapter 1: *How to Hold Yourself Accountable For Everything That You Do* ..39
Chapter 2: How To Deal With Uncertainty? 42
Chapter 3: **How Decluttering Brings You Happiness?** 45
Chapter 4: Happy People Use Their Character Strengths 51
Chapter 5: Happy People Surround Themselves with The Right People
.... 54
Chapter 6: *Five Habits That Can Make Someone Like You* 57
Chapter 7: Happy People Reward Themselves 61
Chapter 8: Don't Stay At Home 65
Chapter 9: Happy People Spend Time Alone 69
Chapter 10: *8 Ways On How To Start Taking Actions* 72
PART 3 77
Chapter 1: *7 Ways To Attract Happiness* 78
Chapter 2: Happy People Plan Their Week in Advance for Maximum Productivity 82
Chapter 3: *5 Scientific Tricks To Become Perfectly Happy* 84

Chapter 4: Happy People Focus on What They Are Good at................ 88

Chapter 5: *7 Ways On How To Attract Success In Life* 92

Chapter 6: Constraints Make You Better: Why the Right Limitations Boost Performance.. 96

10 Habits of Bernard Arnault 99

Chapter 7: Happy People Only Focus on What Is Within Their Control 104

Chapter 8: Happy People Are Busy but Not Rushed 109

Chapter 9: Being 100% Happy Is Overrated... 111

Chapter 10: 5 Lessons on Being Wrong... 115

PART 1

Chapter 1:
Happy People Stay Present

"Realize deeply that the present moment is all you ever have."

According to a study, 50% of the time, we are not fully present in the moment. We are either thinking about the past or worrying about the future. These things lead to frustration, anxiety, and pain in our daily life. Each morning as soon as we wake up, we start seeking distractions. As we wake up with a clear mind, we should be grateful for a new day that we got; instead, we start looking for our phone, start going through interwebs and rush into our days. So now we are going to help you and list some of the things that will help you stay present.

Stop Being a Slave to Your Mind: For the next four days, let's do an exercise where you pay attention to your thoughts and see what crosses your mind. You. You will soon realize that majority of the thoughts that you have are destructive. There will be very little time to think about the present, and the majority of your thoughts would be about the past or the future. So, whenever this happens and you find yourself wandering consciously, try to bring yourself back to the present. Also, you need to remind yourself that multi-tasking is a myth and focus on one thing only.

Tap into Your Senses: If you mindfully tap into your senses, you will realize that it is a fantastic way of bringing more awareness into your day. Because our eyes are wide open all day, we can see, but we forget to tap into other senses such as taste, touch, or smell. But if you use these, you can feel more present and calm down if you are in a stressful situation. You might not realize this, but our senses play a huge role in manifesting our reality. For example, everything we are hearing we are touching will regularly turn into our reality. That is why we can use the power our senses have and feel more calm and present.

Listen Closely: Everyone loves to talk, but only a few people like to listen. People love to share their dreams, what they have accomplished and what they desire, and still, nobody seems to be listening closely.

"When you talk, you are only repeating what you already know. But if you listen, you may learn something new."

When you listen carefully, you will be able to charm people and at the same time learn new things and be present. Because you will be focusing on what they are saying, you will focus on the current moment. This way, you will also be able to silence your thoughts about the past and future because you will be consciously listening and focusing on what they are saying. This will also benefit your relationship in the long run because when you need an ear to listen to your problems, they will be there for you. This is a win-win situation for you, and you will improve your relationship while practising being more present.

Happy People Dream Big

Remember being a kid, and when somebody asked you what you wanted to be after growing up, you answered with a big dream: an astronaut, a ballerina, a scientist, a firefighter, or the President of the United States. You believed that you could achieve anything you set your mind at that no dream is too big that if you wanted, you would make it happen. But why is it that so many adults forget what it is like to dream big. Happy people are dreamers; if you want to become a happy person, you need to make dreaming big a habit; some people even say that if your dreams do not scare you, you are not dreaming big. Now you must be wondering how dreaming big can make you happy. Firstly, it helps you see that if you had a magic wand and you could get whatever you wanted, what you would want for yourself, and there is a chance that these dreams are things you want to achieve in your life somehow other. Secondly, it will help you in removing any fears you have about not being able to achieve your dreams because when you dream big, you think about what you want in your ideal world, and your fear will not come in your way because you would feel like you are living in that fantasy world. Lastly, you will put your dreams and desires into the universe, and the likelihood of making those dreams come true increases. Fulfilling your dreams makes you happy because you will be able to get what you have yearned for so long, and a sense of achievement will make you feel confident about yourself and the dream you had. Now you must have a question what should I do to start dreaming big I am going to outline some of the things you can practice!

Sit back, clear your mind and think about your desires and dreams. What do you want in life? If you had three wishes from a genie, what are the things you would ask for? What is something you would if no one was looking or if you weren't afraid. Now write these dreams down on a piece of paper. This way, they would seem more real. The next thing you should do is start reading some inspirational books that motivate you to start living your best life starting today! Lastly, make a list of goals you want to achieve and start working on them.

Chapter 2:
Don't Wait Another Second To Live Your Dreams

We often think we must be ready to act , but the truth is we will never be ready while we wait.

We only become ready by walking the path, and battles are seldom won in ideal circumstances.

Money is not the real currency in life , the real currency is time and every second we wait is a second we waste.

Your biggest motivator is the ticking clock and the impending reality that one day it will be too late.

Your biggest fear is getting to 80 and realising you haven't lived, that you haven't done what you wanted in life because of fear.

True regret is a medicine none of us want to taste.

We must decide what we really want, set the bar high , go after it now and accept nothing less.

You deserve respect, but you will live what you expect, this life will pay you any price but it's up to you what you accept.

You must act now from where we are with what we have , right now , not tomorrow or next week , right now.

Take the first step , make the draft plan .

Find out what knowledge you need to make this dream a reality.

Taking action now towards the goal in mind is crucial, if we wait we risk losing the drive to make things happen.

We can never be fully ready because we don't know what exactly is going to happen, a lot of it is learned along the way - especially if you're doing something brand new.

Happy Who? Happy You!

If not, reading what has been done before in your area will give you a good understanding of what might work.

Every second we spend thinking about, instead of acting towards our goal is wasted time.

You cannot afford to wait because if you do not act , someone else will , someone else could also be thinking what you're thinking and act first.

Those who wait for opportunity will wait in vain because opportunity must be created, first in the mind, then in the world.

We cannot see the vast opportunity that surrounds us unless we believe it is there, believe it is possible and act on that belief, at the time it arises.

The world is pliable and opportunities do not wait for people to be ready.

You must become ready on the road.

The obstacles you have to overcome on the move will mould you into the person you need to be to reach your biggest goals.

You must be patient, to be practitioners of who you believe you will be one day.

Getting into the mindset of whoever you want to be right now, because until you become that person in mind, you cannot in body.

As we start acting differently, different actions bring different results and if the new actions are positive and aimed at a certain goal , just like magic the world begins to transform for you, towards the life you wanted.

The leap of faith is acting now, feeling unready aiming for something that may seem unrealistic, but this is an essential leap and test to be overcome.

As the days go on with the goal in mind , it will seem to become more likely and you will feel more ready until it feels definite.

All things are possible but there will be required ingredients to your success you might not know yet, so the first step is to gain the knowledge required.

Once you begin to learn that knowledge you are on the road to your goal.

Organization and optimization of your time will make it easier to be efficient.

If time is the real currency, are you getting good value for what you spend your time doing?

If not , is it not time you used some of your seconds working towards something phenomenal?

Happy Who? Happy You!

You only have so many and it is losing value every day as we age, think about it.

We must create a sense of urgency because it is urgent if you want to succeed in an ever changing world.

If we wait our ideas, products and services may become irrelevant because new technology and innovation is always changing.

Our ideas are only viable when they come ,

Strike while the iron is hot is good advice ,

When the ambition and goal is strongest and clearest.

Clarity is essential when pursuing dreams and goals, every detail of your dream should be clear in your mind down to the sights , colours and smells.

When we think about our goal we should feel it as if it's already here, and start acting like it is.

Dress talk and walk as if you are that person now.

Whatever our current circumstances everyone has the ability to build in their minds, set the goal then determine the first step.

If your circumstances are bad there are more steps, but there are steps.

Start from step one and walk in confidence always keeping the big dream in mind knowing that this can happen for you.

We have a waking mind and a subconscious mind.

The subconscious knows things we don't, it is responsible for our gut instinct, which always seems to be right so follow that .

Everyday listening to that voice , keeping a clear vision of your goal in your mind and confidently taking action towards it.

It's possible for you if you act ,

But time is ticking.

Chapter 3:
Why You Need To Find Your Why

Your why is your reason for being.

Your reason for living.

Your reason for acting.

Without a why life begins to feel demoralising.

Without a purpose, what is the purpose?

What chance do you think you have of achieving anything, without a reason?

Go out and ask 20 people why they are working, apart from the pay.

Roughly 16 will not be able to give you a clear answer, and 4 will.

The 4 that will have a plan and a goal to achieve more.

They probably already are more successful than the 16 with no answer.

The 4 know their current work is just a step to a bigger goal.

They know their what and their why behind everything they are doing.

The 16 just landed in that job by chance and will probably never leave it.

They may progress up the company ladder slowly,

But with no clear reason to achieve anything greater they will stay where they are, in perceived security.

Do you know why you are doing what you are doing?

If not, it's about time you discover your why.

It may be to providing a better life for your family and friends.

Your motives may be financial, they may not.

Maybe your why is to lead a less stressful life.

Happy Who? Happy You!

Maybe that means your require less money to be happy.

Your reason is individual and personal.
No one else should influence that.
Seek to heed advice from people who are where you want to be in life.
You wouldn't let a mechanic perform surgery on you,
so why would you accept advice on success from the unsuccessful.

They may be successful in their field.
But if their field is not your field, they have no business telling you how to play.
Their why is not your why, and their what is not your what.
If the goals and reasons are different, the advice is irrelevant.

Politely respect their advice.
Use their success to fuel your drive for success in your own field.
Help it guide you to a similar path that you are aiming towards.

Your why is so important.
It will be the reason you persist when things get tough.
If you have no clearly defined reason, it becomes easy for you to quit.

A clearly defined goal (your what),
and a clearly defined reason (your why),
are critical to any lasting happiness and success.
Without them you are just aimlessly drifting from nothing to nothing.
Without clearly defining the terms of your life , you forfeit the power of your will and your life will be decided by someone else.
That is tragedy.

Your why truly is everything on the path to achieving your what.
Your end goal.
Your dream life.

Happy Who? Happy You!

Everything that you will sit down and clearly define.

The detail of everything and the people who will enjoy it - your ultimate why.

What and why go together like salt and pepper or bread and butter.

You can't have one without the other.

Chapter 4:
Why Helping Others Can Make You Happier

A Chinese saying goes, "If you want happiness for an hour, take a nap. If you want happiness for a day, go fishing. If you want happiness for a year, inherit a fortune. If you want happiness for a lifetime, help somebody." So many great thinkers have emphasized finding happiness in helping others. Thus we learn early: It is more competent to offer than to get. The admired truism is drummed into our heads from our first cut of a birthday cake. Yet, is there a more profound truth behind the axiom?

The reverberating answer is yes. Scientific research gives convincing information to help the narrative prove that giving is an amazing pathway to self-awareness and enduring joy. Through fMRI innovation, we currently realize that giving activates the very pieces of the mind that are stimulated by sex and food. Experts show proof that benevolence is designed in mind—and it's pleasurable. Helping other people may simply be the key to carrying on with a daily existence that isn't just more joyful yet in addition better, richer, more useful, and significant. Here are some tips that will help you give not until it hurts but until it feels great:

1. Give To Organizations With Transparent Aims and Results
As indicated by Harvard researcher Michael Norton, "Providing for the reason that determines how they will manage your cash prompts more

bliss than providing for an umbrella reason where you're not entirely certain where your not sure where your cash is going

2. Find Ways to Integrate Your Interests and Skills With The Necessities of Others

"Selfless giving, without self-safeguarding senses, effectively gets overpowering," says Adam Grant, creator of Giving and Take. It is essential to Be "otherish," which he characterizes as being willing to give more than you get, yet at the same time keeping your own advantages insight.

3. Give your time

The endowment of time is regularly more important to the recipient and more fulfilling for the giver than the endowment of cash. We don't all have a similar measure of cash. However, we as a whole have time to burn and can give a portion of this chance to help other people—regardless of whether that implies we dedicate our lifetimes to support or simply allow a couple of hours every day or a couple of days a year.

Chapter 5:
How to Reprogram Your Mind for Success

Your routines are the things that drive you through life. Your routines are driven by your emotions. Your emotions are a sum of your past. Your past is a sum of incidents. These incidents may be related to a person or a thing, which in turn make your life exciting.

You start your day with a thought. A thought that wakes you up every day. A unique thought that everyone experiences every morning. These thoughts are the driving force for you to get up whether you like it or not.

These thoughts may be fear-driven or love memories. So your brain creates emotions in your subconscious mind which in turn dictates your daily tasks and routine.

You might be having doubts about a leave from a job that you might deserve because you can't get the doubt of getting fired out of your mind.

You might be remembering a loved one that you want to see today.

You may be hoping to get some good news today.

So you have a set routine every day, that you follow without even ever pondering on day-to-day life. And this is the ultimate failure of your purpose in life.

A routine that is not getting you forward in life isn't worth living with. But you are not able to think about it because your mind and your subconscious have taken over your body.

As all these obvious things are being stated, close your eyes, put some music on, shut the doors or sit on a bench in a quiet part. Tell your mind to get rid of those memories that drive your emotions. Leave your body motionless and try to take deep breaths.

As you start doing this, you will feel an immediate thought kick in your subconscious. Your mind will be making you feel like something is missing or if you had something to do.

This is an uncomfortable state of mind. But now is your time to be your own master. Tell your subconscious that it is your will that leads you, but not the emotions and your mind.

You have to realize the reality and make it seem more acceptable to your brain. You have to make it feel confident and feel that it is helping you to stay commited in any situation that comes across in your life.

You need to become conscious in this hectic world of involuntary unconsciousness.

You have to make yourself ready for the unpredictable future. Because if you are not ready for the future, you are still drowning in your past.

Everyone's past is toxic. Even good memories can be toxic. One might ask how.

The memories of the past either make your stay in the bed or they make you hope full of chances to come with luck. But luck is rarely lucky.

You cannot be a free man till you dive out of your personal reality that your brain has created to keep you in your comfort zone. You cannot become successful if you stay on your laptop or your phone interacting with the world via social media and emails.

You have to create your own environment by making new friends, taking new jobs, asking questions to your partner, making a change in your natural habitat.

Your mind is the curator of your environment and the people in it. So you have to change your environment by making your mind commit to your orders.

Give your mind a free space to rehabilitate and renew itself. Give it a chance to imagine new things. Make it wander off like a herd of cattle in the grasslands. Let it flow without any emotion, just to create enough space for new realities to pop in. As soon as it does, you will find yourself in a new realm of happiness and success.

Chapter 6:
The Downside of Work-Life Balance

One way to think about work-life balance is with a concept known as The Four Burners Theory. Here's how it was first explained to me:

Imagine that a stove represents your life with four burners on it. Each burner symbolizes one major quadrant of your life.

1. The first burner represents your family.
2. The second burner is your friends.
3. The third burner is your health.
4. The fourth burner is your work.

The Four Burners Theory says that "to be successful, you have to cut off one of your burners. And to be successful, you have to cut off two."

The View of the Four Burners

My initial reaction to The Four Burners Theory was to search for a way to bypass it. "Can I succeed and keep all four burners running?" I wondered.

Perhaps I could combine two burners. "What if I lumped family and friends into one category?"

Maybe I could combine health and work. "I hear sitting all day is unhealthy. What if I got a standing desk?" Now, I know what you are thinking. Believing that you will be healthy because you bought a standing desk is like believing you are a rebel because you ignored the fasten seatbelt sign on an airplane, but whatever.

Soon I realized I was inventing these workarounds because I didn't want to face the real issue: life is filled with tradeoffs. If you want to excel in your work and your marriage, then your friends and your health may have to suffer. If you want to be healthy and succeed as a parent, then you might be forced to dial back your career ambitions. Of course, you are free to divide your time equally among all four burners, but you have to accept that you will never reach your full potential in any given area.

Essentially, we are forced to choose. Would you rather live a life that is unbalanced but high-performing in a certain area? Or would you rather live a life that is balanced but never maximizes your potential in a given quadrant?

Option 1: Outsource Burners

We outsource small aspects of our lives all the time. We buy fast food, so we don't have to cook. We go to the dry cleaners to save time on laundry. We visit the car repair shop, so we don't have to fix our automobile.

Outsourcing small portions of your life allow you to save time and spend it elsewhere. Can you apply the same idea to one quadrant of your life and free up time to focus on the other three burners?

Work is the best example. For many people, work is the hottest burner on the stove. It is where they spend the most time, and it is the last burner to get turned off. In theory, entrepreneurs and business owners can outsource the work burner. They do it by hiring employees.

The Four Burners Theory reveals a truth everyone must deal with: nobody likes being told they can't have it all, but everyone has constraints on their time and energy. Every choice has a cost.

Which burners have you cut off?

Chapter 7:
How to Eat With Mood in Mind

At the point when you're feeling down, it tends to be enticing to go to food to lift your spirits. Notwithstanding, the sweet, fatty treats that numerous individuals resort to have unfortunate results of their own. Along these lines, you may puzzle over whether any good food sources can work on your temperament.

As of late, research on the connection between sustenance and psychological wellness has been arising. However, note that state of mind can be impacted by numerous variables, like pressure, climate, helpless rest, hereditary qualities, mood disorders, and nutritional deficiencies. In any case, certain food varieties have been displayed to further develop general mental wellbeing and specific kinds of temperament issues.

1. Fatty Fish

Omega-3 unsaturated fats are a gathering of fundamental fats you should get through your eating routine because your body can't produce them all alone. Fatty fish like salmon and tuna fish are wealthy in two sorts of omega-3s — docosahexaenoic corrosive (DHA) and eicosapentaenoic corrosive (EPA) — that are connected to bring down degrees of despair. Omega-3s add to lower your depression and seem to assume key parts in mental health and cell flagging.

2. Dark Chocolate

Chocolate is wealthy in numerous mood-boosting compounds. Its sugar may further develop mood since it's a fast wellspring of fuel for your brain. Besides, it's anything but a course of feel-great mixtures, like caffeine, theobromine, and N-acylethanolamine — a substance synthetically like cannabinoids that have been connected to improved mood.

3. Fermented Food Varieties

Fermented food sources, which incorporate kimchi, yogurt, kefir, fermented tea, and sauerkraut, may further develop gut wellbeing and state of mind. The fermentation interaction permits live microbes to flourish in food varieties ready to change over sugars into liquor and acids. During this interaction, probiotics are made. These live microorganisms support the development of solid microscopic organisms in your gut and may expand serotonin levels.

4. Bananas

Bananas may assist with flipping around a frown.

They're high in nutrient B6, which orchestrates feel-great synapses like dopamine and serotonin.

Moreover, one enormous banana (136 grams) gives 16 grams of sugar and 3.5 grams of fiber.

When matched with fiber, sugar is delivered gradually into your circulation system, considering stable glucose levels and better disposition control. Glucose levels that are too low may prompt irritability and emotional episodes.

5. Oats

Oats are an entire grain that can keep you feeling great the entire morning. You can appreciate them in numerous structures, like, for the time being, oats, oatmeal, muesli, and granola. They're a phenomenal wellspring of fiber, giving 8 grams in a solitary crude cup (81 grams). Fiber eases back your processing of carbs, considering a slow arrival of sugar into the circulation system to keep your energy levels stable.

Chapter 8:
Playing To Your Strengths

Have you ever asked yourself why you fail at everything you touch?
Why you seem to lack behind everyone you strive to beat?
Why you can't give up the things that are keeping you from achieving the goals you dream?
Has anyone told you the reason for all this?

You might wonder about it all your life and might never get to the right answer. Even though you stare at the answer every day in the mirror.

Yes! It's you! You are the reason for your failures.
You are the reason for everything bad going on in your life right now.
But you are also the master of your life, and you should start acting like one.

When the world brings you down, find another way to overcome the pressures.
Find another way to beat the odds.
Adverse situations only serve to challenge you.
Be mentally strong and bring the world to your own game.

Show the world what you are.
Show the world what you are capable of.

Happy Who? Happy You!

Don't let anyone dictate to you what you should do.
Rather shape your life to dictate the outcome with your efforts and skills.

You can't always be wrong.
Somewhere, and somehow, you will get the right answer.
That will be your moment to build what you lost.
That will be your moment to shut everyone else and rise high in the silence of your opponents.

If you don't get that chance, don't wait for it to come.
Keep going your way and keep doing the things you do best.
Paths will open to your efforts one day.

You can't be bad at everything you do.
You must be good at something.
Find out what works for you.
Find out what drives your spirit.
Find out what you can do naturally while being blind-folded with your hands tied behind your back.

There is something out there that is calling out to you.
Once you find it, be the best at it as you can.
It doesn't matter if you do not get to the top.
You don't anything to prove to anyone.
You only need one glimpse of positivity to show yourself that you have something worthwhile to live for.

Always challenge yourself.

If you did 5 hours of work today, do 7 tomorrow.

If you run 1 mile today, hit 3 by the end of the week.

You know exactly what you are capable of.

Play to your strengths.

Make it your motto to keep going every single day.

Make a decision.

Be decisive.

Stick with it.

Don't be afraid because there is nothing to fear.

The only thing to fear is the fear itself.

Tell your heart and your mind today, that you can't stop, and you won't stop.

Till the time you have the last breath in your lungs and the last beat in your heart, keep going.

You will need to put your heart out to every chance you can get to raise yourself from all this world and be invincible.

You have no other option but to keep going.

To keep trying until you have broken all the barriers to freedom.

You are unique and you know it.

You just need to have the guts to admit that you are special and live up to the person you were always meant to be.

Take stock of yourself today.

Happy Who? Happy You!

Where are you right now and where do you want to be?
The moment you realize your true goal, that is the moment you have unlocked your strengths.

Live your life on your terms.
Every dream that you dream is obtainable.
And the only way is to believe in yourself.
To believe that you are the only thing standing in the way of your past and your future.

Once you have started, tell yourself that there is no return.
Dictate your body to give up only when you have crossed the finish line.

Start acting on every whim that might get you to the ultimate fate.
These whims are your strength because you have them for a purpose.

Why walk when you can run?
Why run when you can fly?
Why listen when you can sing?
Why go out and dine when you can cook?

The biggest gift that you can give to yourself is the mental satisfaction that you provide yourself.
You are only limited to the extent you cage yourself.
The time you let go will be your salvation. But you have to let go!

Chapter 9:
Overcoming Fear and Self-Doubt

The lack of belief most people have is the reason for their failure at even the smallest things in life. The biggest killer of dreams is the lack of belief in ourselves and the doubt of failure.

We all make mistakes. We all have some ghosts of the past that haunt us. We all have something to hide. We all have something that we regret. But what you are today is not the result of your mistakes.

You are here because of your struggles to make those things go away. You are here now with the power and strength to shape your present and your future.

Our mind is designed to take the shape of what we hold long enough inside it. The things we frequently think about ultimately start filling in the spaces within our memory, so we have to be careful. We have to decide whether we want to stay happy or to hold on to the fear we once wanted to get rid of.

The human spirit and human soul are colored by the impressions we ourselves decide to impose.

The reason why we don't want to explore the possibility of what to do is that subconsciously we don't believe that it can happen for us. We don't believe that we deserve it or if it was meant for us.

So here is something I suggest. Ask yourself, how much time in a day do you spend thinking about your dream? How much time do you spend working on your dreams everyday? What books did you read this year? What new skills have you acquired recently? What have you done that makes you worthy of your dream? Nothing?

Then you are on point with your doubt because you don't have anything to show for when the opportunity presents itself.

You don't succeed because you have this latent fear. Fear that makes you think about the consequences of what will happen if you fail even with all the good things on your hand?

I know that feeling but failure is there to teach you one important and maybe the most essential skill life can teach us; Resilience.

You rediscover your life once you have the strength to fight your every fear and every doubt because you have better things on your hand to care for.

You have another dream to pursue. Another horizon awaits you. Another peak to summit. It doesn't matter if you literally have to run to stand still. You got to do what you got to do, no matter the consequences and the sacrifices.

But failing to do what is required of you has no justifiable defense. Not even fear. Because your fears are self-imposed and you already have many wrong things going on for you right now.

Don't let fear be one of them. Because fear is the most subtle and destructive disease So inhale all your positive energies and exhale all your doubts because you certainly are a better person without them.

Chapter 10:
How to Share Your Talent

Hi everybody! I hope everyone is doing well. Today, we're going to talk about sharing your talent to the world. As humans, it is so natural to us to feel that we want to share a part of ourselves to the world around us through one way or another. We have this yearning to create or produce something that will benefit other people. We feel a sense of fulfillment in knowing that we did something to positively impact other people's lives. And one way to do this is by sharing our talents.

So, let's get to the steps on how you'll be able to share your talents.

First, you have to discover your talent. Know what you can offer. Believe that you have something in you that you can offer to the world to be the light that it needs and find it. Listen to your intuition and subconscious mind. Most of the time, your intuition knows what you have and how you'll be able to let it out. Know that everyone is unique and the world needs your authenticity and whatever that you can give. Don't allow society or cultural norms to dictate what you should be doing or where you should be good at.

Next, practice what you believe you're good at. Discovering your talents doesn't always mean that you'll be instantly great at it. You still need to make efforts to hone them. Take your time to practice and focus on your progress. Even the most talented musicians or athletes that ever walk this on planet spent so much time practicing and improving their crafts. So, don't give up if you feel like you are not going anywhere with your talent.

Third step is to be open to all possibilities. Sometimes, we want to be really good at one thing and we end up not giving ourselves a chance to be open to other opportunities. Life is full of surprises. Don't limit yourself in one field because you won't know what are the other things you're good at if you'll be so afraid to try something new. You're probably pursuing to hone your talent in music but you might also be good in writing. You won't know that you write really well if you don't give yourself a chance to try it. So, be open to all the possibilities and don't ever hold back.

Next step is to find your tribe. Your tribe is the people that share the same visions as you. They are the ones that believe in you and support you in your endeavors as you hone your talents. They make you feel that you and your talents are valued. And you do all these to them too. You support one another. Being with the right people that empower you to realize your full potential is an important part of your journey. So, if you'll ever find your tribe, stay with them and you'll surely go places.

Fifth step is to get yourself out in the world. Don't hesitate to show yourself and what you can offer. Remember that there's only one you in the whole world and that is your power. Even if some people will reject you and your work, there will always be people that you will inspire by just merely showing up. Don't let every rejection stop you in sharing your talent. Many successful authors have faced multiple rejections before their works got published. A lot of great actors and actresses have experienced failed auditions before they get to perform in televisions and cinemas. Many engineers have received bad grades when they were students before they got their degree. But they all made it to where they are now because they did not let any of the rejections they received to stop them in honing their talents and pursuing their dreams. So, don't give up on your talents. With perseverance and hardwork, you will also shine and light someone's world.

When you share your talent, you're not only making a positive impact on other people's lives but it also improves your own being. There is no other more fulfilling feeling in the world than to know that you've made someone's day a little brighter by sharing a part of yourself. As humans, we only have one chance to walk on this planet. And if we could make this world a little better than how we find it, that one chance is totally worth it. Life is beautiful as they say. But it will be even better if we share it

Happy Who? Happy You!

with others.

I hope today's video will move you to start sharing your talent. If you like this, give this a thumbs up and subscribe to my channel for more. I'll see you on the next one!

PART 2

Chapter 1:
How to Hold Yourself Accountable For Everything That You Do

Staying on top of your work can be difficult without a manager over your shoulder. So how exactly do you manage yourself? I don't know about you, but I have a problem. I am ambitious; I am full of great ideas. I am also, however, extremely undisciplined. But the other day, I had an idea. What if I became "my manager"? Not a bad idea.

Contrary to what the multi-million dollar management training industry says, I don't think management is rocket science (though I am not saying it is easy). A good manager motivates and supports people and makes people accountable. To manage ourselves, we simply need to take concrete steps to motivate ourselves and make ourselves accountable.

1. **Create a Personal Mission Statement**

I think we get so caught up in the mundane details of daily life that we often lose track of why we're here, what we want, and, most importantly, what we value. Manage yourself by finding a way to integrate your values into what you do. Write your mission statement.

My mission statement, at the moment, is this: "To live simply and give selflessly, and to work diligently towards financial independence and the opportunities such independence will afford me."

Your mission statement doesn't have to be profound or poetic – it just needs to convey your core values and define why you do what you do each day. (Hint: If you can't find a mission statement that fits your current career or life, maybe it is time for a change!

2. Set Micro-Goals

There are countless benefits to writing down goals of all sizes. Annual, five-, and ten-year goals can help you expand on your mission statement because you know you are working towards a tangible result. But long-term goals are useless unless you have a strategy to achieve them. Manage yourself by setting micro-goals.

What is a micro-goal? I like to think of it as a single action that, when accomplished, serves as a building block to a much larger goal.

For example, the resolution to make a larger-than minimum monthly payment on a credit card balance is a micro goal. Each month you successfully increase your payment, you are closer to your big goal of getting out of debt.

At work, a micro-goal might involve setting up an important client meeting. Getting all the elements for a meeting in place is one step towards a larger goal of winning or increasing a particular business relationship.

A micro goal is not, however, anything that goes on your to-do list. Responding to a customer inquiry or cleaning out your cubicle is not a micro-goal unless, of course, you have bigger goals to specifically involving that customer or to get more organized.

Chapter 2:
How To Deal With Uncertainty?

How many of you are going through life right now but are dealing with a load of uncertainty that is weighing heavily on your mind?

You could be worrying about your career or work related matters: you wonder because the economy is taking a hit, whether you will still have your job tomorrow, whether your business would survive, or even if the economy is good, you are uncertain if you quit the current job you hate whether you are able to find another job in the near future or if you will even be competent in your new profession.

Or you could be worrying about your loved ones, your child who is studying overseas, or your spouse where they are working in the healthcare profession, working in the police or fire department, or even the military, where their lives are put at risk every single day, you worry if there will be one day that you might lose them and they won't come home.

Or you could be uncertain about smaller matters, matters such as if your date went well and if they would give you a call to ask you out again.

Whatever these may be, they all fall under the umbrella of uncertainty.

I would like to share with you uncertainties I faced personally and I would like to provide you with action steps to deal with them.

Recently I had been struggling with many uncertainties in my life. While they might not be your struggles I believe I would be able to provide more value if i shared my own story.

Happy Who? Happy You!

The first uncertainty I had was that I had recently restarted my publishing business after being away from it for a year, I was so afraid of what the market condition was like now, I was afraid of the competition, I was afraid I would fail again. I was afraid I would waste more of my time building up a business only to have it taken away from me.

The second worry I had was that I had also just begun taking my real estate exam to become a licensed realtor. I started having doubts about myself that I would ever become a competent realtor like my peers and I would look like a fool and I would feel disappointed with myself thereafter.

The next uncertainty I had was whether I would get the jobs that I applied for. I had decided to take on a part or full-time position to grow my professional career and I was afraid Whether the hours I spent on job applications would be in vain and that i would get no responses or even worse, rejections.

The final uncertainty was with stocks. Due to the incredible market volatility, I couldn't sleep properly every night because I wasn't sure what was gonna happen tmr. Whether I was gonna lose money while i was asleep.

I went about days with all these negative thoughts looming in my mind. It affected my sleep, my well-being, and my happiness. I started becoming dreary, unhappy, and lifeless. I spent 80% of my waking hours with these fears and doubts, and constantly beating myself up for feeling this way and it only made matters worse.

One day I decided it was enough. I took a deep breath and started collecting myself. I had had enough and I was so done with feeling these uncertainty and feeling sorry for myself.

I made the decision to accept my struggles, that they were a part of life and that there was no point in worrying about it. I decided it that I would just work hard on these areas, keep doing my best, and that whatever outcomes doesn't matter because I've given it my all. And finally I decided to live my day to the fullest and just be grateful that I even get to have the opportunity to pursue these ventures. After going through this process day in and day out, I became more at peace with myself. I started feeling less anxiety and adopted a more optimistic and positive mindset.

Here's what I realized. Uncertainty is born out of fear. This could be fear of losing someone, fear of the unknown, or even fear of failure. I had immense fears of failure that it crippled me to a really low point in my life. And the only way to overcome fear is first to accept that it is normal to be fearful, and then after to not let that fear get in the way of your happiness because life is too short for you to spend in a state of fearfulness. Rather, spend your time feeling grateful for your life and just try your best in everything that you do. Keep working on your dreams as if it were your last day on this earth, keep loving your spouse or child as though it was their last day on this earth, and ask yourself, is this how you would want to spend your time letting fear and uncertainty feed on your happiness? Or would you rather cherish every single moment you have with yourself and your family, and to live life with abundance instead.

This is my challenge to you. Uncertainty can only cripple you if you let it. Focus on your journey, your path, and trust in the process. But most importantly, Trust in yourself, believe in yourself even if no one else will. You owe that much love and compassion to yourself. I know you can do it.

Chapter 3:
How Decluttering Brings You Happiness?

You must have heard people telling you about how decluttering benefited them in numerous ways. Some even exaggerate to say that it changed their lives entirely. But in today's fast world, everything is easy and quick - everything, but happiness. Happiness is not something we can just expect to have, but we can take steps to attain it as much as possible.

Today we're going to talk about how decluttering can help bring some of that happy state of mind into our lives. While it might sound tedious to think about decluttering your space, it has many wonderful benefits that can only be experienced once you begin the process.

Here are 7 Ways that decluttering can bring you happiness.

Keeping your stuff organized makes you calm

If you say that a messy area is where you can feel more comfortable then most likely, you haven't experienced what a clean area can really do for you. It is human nature that we find peace in places and things that are organized and sorted. Take for example your bed - If you come back home to a made bed, you'll instantly feel relaxed seeing how your sheets and pillows are where they should be. But if they are strewn all over the place, you will find yourself in a fix.

In decluttering, you organize your stuff and place all your items where they should be. Each having a purpose and a place for being there. No excess, no extra items where they bring about a chaotic state of mind. Less is often more in this case. Consider packing up the excess stuff that takes up room on your desk, and either keep them in storage or consider placing them somewhere else where it does not interfere with the space that you are trying to keep organized.

I found it! The happiness of finding something new."

The Polaroid that slipped under your mattress and that pendant your mom gave you at the last family meet-up. Many such things are often lost in our rooms and homes - Items that you've either completely forgotten about, or items that you never even knew existed in the first place. Decluttering, by taking a methodical approach - cupboard by cupboard, shelf by shelf, and drawer by drawer, allows you to be extremely thorough. To the point where you might find hidden gems if the last time you did so was when you first moved in to the house.

After all, what's better than finding your things that can potentially bring back memories? The joy you might feel is something that you should be excited about. Gifts, treasures, and even money could be on the list of items that you may find.

This trip down memory lane brings back memories.

This may sound poetic but it is real. When you declutter and you go through your things piece by piece, you will inevitably come across loads of time capsule items such as your high school diary, pile of letters from past friendships that you saved when you were young, or even love letters from past admirers and past relationships. All of these things will bring you back in time when things were simpler, and you will experience the emotions as you go through all these relics once again as if you were receiving it for the first time.

You may even start to wonder what ever happened to those friends of the past – to wonder how they are doing right now, and to rekindle old friendships that time has stolen from us.

So many times we don't even realize what we need, and maybe all we need is just a reminder you have had so many wonderful memories leading up to this day. Happy memories that help you realize that you will have many more wonderful memories ahead as well. Those events of happiness and warmth are lying in the corner of your room, waiting for you to open them.

There is nothing more essential than letting go of negativity.

Who can agree that negativity is on the top of the list of the things we don't need in life. When you declutter and start sorting things out, you are also actively engaging in the process of sorting the negative energy too. You hold in the palm of your hands items that don't bring you joy, items that don't bring you happiness, and you make a conscious decision to put them aside or discard them away. At the same time you could be releasing anger, anxiety, sadness, and more from your space, leaving more room for happiness to flow in.

To Make Room For Space

To continue from the previous point, letting go of things that don't serve a purpose anymore will give you more freedom to enjoy the space you are working or living in. Decluttering does not mean that you can now acquire more things to fill up those gaps. Doing so defeats the purpose of clearing stuff out in the first place. Instead choose to leave your space empty unless something really compelling comes along that you simply cannot live without. What you may not realise is that having less things actually makes us feel happier than more.

Having more things means that we are never satisfied with how things are. It means having to spend more money to buy those things, working longer hours, and never really being at peace with just having enough stuff. We want to make room for the things that matter to us. Things that serve us rather become a slave to it. Choose your items wisely if you must, otherwise it is perfectly fine the way it is, clutter-free.

Getting rid of clutter can boost your productivity

A clear space equals a clear mind. Having a clean work desk or work environment serves as inspiration for us to create new and exciting things. When we see that pile of stuff in the corner, attention is always drawn away from us unexpectedly. This distraction shifts our focus from being productive into one of annoyance. Instead, consider placing only items that serve to motivate you and encourage you to chase your dreams. For example, either a motivational quote by a famous artist, photos of successful people you want to emulate, or even a vision board that you create for yourself. Things that create a deep and emotional reaction in you to make you want to be more productive. Chuck those ornaments and junk to one side and make room for these invaluable items.

To Invite More Positive Energy Into Your Space

When we learn to live with less things, we also subconsciously live in a state of abundance. Abundance in the sense that we disassociate having things with happiness. We untie ourselves from the notion that having more means increased happiness.

By only making room for the best things in our homes, we allocate our spending on one essential item that we designate to a specific area. For example our couch or television. One that know we will love to use every single time we come home. We don't feel a need to buy another one just to fill up an empty space just because it is there. We buy one great desk and work chair to encourage us to be productive, and so on and so forth. Everything having a purpose and a place to be there.

Having more space also invites positivity because we allow ourselves the freedom to move around our house with ease. Not bumping into things, not having to maneuver in a weird fashion just to avoid a furniture. We flow freely from one room to the next. That is the ultimate goal that we should all try to achieve when we embark on the process of decluttering.

Conclusion…

This world gives us a lot of things to maintain and live for and somewhere in this race, we forget that we are alive. This feeling of heartbreak and misery will never consume you if you keep taking care of yourself. Decluttering is an essential part of that act of looking after yourself. So invite more happiness into your life by decluttering… love yourself more and enjoy the sunlight of your life.

Chapter 4:
Happy People Use Their Character Strengths

One of the most popular exercises in the science of positive psychology (some argue it is the single most popular exercise) is referred to as "use your signature strengths in new ways." But what does this exercise mean? How do you make the most of it to benefit yourself and others?

On the surface, the exercise is self-explanatory:

a. Select one of your highest strengths – one of your **character strengths** that is core to who you are, is easy for you to use, and gives you energy;
b. Consider a new way to express the strength each day;
c. Express the strength in a new way each day for at least 1 week.

Studies repeatedly show that this exercise is connected with long-term benefits (e.g., 6 months) such as higher levels of happiness and lower levels of depression.

PUT THE EXERCISE INTO PRACTICE

In practice, however, people sometimes find it surprisingly challenging to come up with new ways to use one of their signature strengths. This is because we are very accustomed to using our strengths. We frequently use our strengths mindlessly without much awareness. For example, have you paid much attention to your use of self-regulation as you brush your teeth? Your level of prudence or kindness while driving? Your humility while at a team meeting?

For some strengths, it is easy to come up with examples. Want to apply **curiosity** in a new way? Below is a sample mapping of what you might do. Keep it simple. Make it complex. It's up to you!

- On Monday, take a new route home from work and explore your environment as you drive.
- On Tuesday, ask one of your co-workers a question you have not previously asked them.
- On Wednesday, try a new food for lunch – something that piques your curiosity to taste.
- On Thursday, call a family member and explore their feelings about a recent positive experience they had.
- On Friday, take the stairs instead of the elevator and explore the environment as you do.
- On Saturday, as you do one household chore (e.g., washing the dishes, vacuuming), pay attention to 3 novel features of the activity while you do it. Example: Notice the whirring sound of the vacuum, the accumulation of dust swirling around in the container, the warmth of the water as you wash the dishes, the sensation of the weight of a single plate or cup, and so on.
- On Sunday, ask yourself 2 questions you want to explore about yourself – reflect or journal your immediate responses.
- Next Monday….keep going!

WIDENING THE SCOPE

In some instances, you might feel challenged to come up with examples. Let me help. After you choose one of your signature strengths, consider the following 10 areas to help jolt new ideas within you and stretch your approach to the strength.

How might I express the character strength…

- At work
- In my closest relationship
- While I engage in a hobby
- When with my friends
- When with my parents or children
- When I am alone at home
- When I am on a team
- As the leader of a project or group
- While I am driving
- While I am eating

Chapter 5:
Happy People Surround Themselves with The Right People

Whether we realized it or not, we become like the five people we spend the most time with. We start behaving like them, thinking like them, looking like them. We even make decisions based on what we think they would want us to do.

For example, there are many research findings that prove we are more likely to gain weight if a close friend or a family member becomes overweight. Similarly, we are more likely to engage in an exercise program if we surround ourselves with fit and health-oriented people.

So, who are the top 5 influencers in your life? Do they make you feel positive? Do they inspire and motivate you to be the best version of yourself? Do they support and encourage you to achieve your goals? Or, do they tell you that "it can't be done," "it's not possible," "you aren't good enough," "you will most likely fail."

If you feel emotionally drained by the energetic vampires in your life, you may want to detox your life and get rid of the relationships that aren't serving you in a positive way.

The negative people, the naysayers, the Debbie Downers, and the chronic complainers are like a dark cloud over your limitless potential.

They hold you back and discourage you from even trying because they're afraid that if you succeed, you'll prove them wrong.

Have the courage to remove the negative people from your life and watch how your energy and enthusiasm automatically blossom. Letting go of the relationships that aren't serving us is a critical step if we want to become more positive, fulfilled, and successful.

Detoxing your life from negative influencers will also allow you to become the person you truly want to be. You'll free yourself from constant judgment, negativity, and lack of support.

Here's what you can do:

- Stay away from chronic complainers.
- Stop participating in meaningless conversations.
- Share your ideas only with people who are supportive or willing to provide constructive criticism.
- Minimize your interactions with "friends," coworkers, and family members who are negative, discouraging, and bitter.
- Stop watching TV and reading negative posts on social media (yes, mainstream media is a major negative influence in our lives!).
- Surround yourself with positive and successful people (remember, we become like the top 5 people we spend our time with!).

- Find new, like-minded friends, join networking and support groups, or find a positive coach or a mentor.

If you want to make a positive change in your life, remember, the people around you have a critical influence on your energy, growth, and probability of success.

Positive people bring out the best in you and make you feel motivated and happy. They help you when you're in need, encourage you to go after your dreams, and are there to celebrate your successes or support you as you move past your challenges. Pick your top 5 wisely!

Chapter 6:
Five Habits That Can Make Someone Like You

Favor and love are won. It is an endless race in life that requires zeal. You have to appeal to the other person so that they can like you back and return some affection. We often struggle to make those around us realize that we like them. Sometimes we succeed and at other times, we learn (not lose). The struggle is real and we need to measure up to the task.

Here are five habits that can make someone like you:

1. **Compliment Them Genuinely**

Do not underestimate the power of a simple compliment on someone. A compliment is an indication that you recognize the other person's excellence in something. Appreciate their dressing, skills, effort or assistance lent to you by saying a 'thank you or you look amazing today!' When you make people feel loved by often genuinely complimenting them, they get motivated and feel loved. Always give genuine compliments and avoid faking them because it may come out as envy or jealousy. Instead of building bridges with the other person, you would have unknowingly built a wall.

Wouldn't you like someone who genuinely compliments you? Of course, you would. The glory that fills your heart when you are complimented will draw you to the other person. Genuine compliments are given in private or public. It is hypocritical to wait to be in public before you compliment someone. There is no occasion for acknowledging another. As long as it is in their presence, do not shy away from it.

2. **Support Their Initiatives**

Be in the front line to support the businesses and initiatives of those you want to court their attention. Be in their cheering squad and support their businesses and careers in whatever capacity. To be able to make someone like you, first court their attention, and what better way is there than to show up in those activities that matter to them?

If you develop the habit of being their ambassador in their businesses, they will see that you both have aligned goals and may take a keen interest in you. Their liking for you will grow as you appreciate their work and interests. Supporting their initiatives also means advising them on matters you are competent in. Your input should not be sycophancy but aimed at making a change.

Those you want to like you will do so in appreciation of your invaluable input in their work. Your ties will be stronger and they will like you more beyond your unconditional support. Be careful to maintain the relationship between you two. It is fragile more so that you are the one initiating it and it is up to them to fall for it.

3. **Stand Up For Them**

What can your friends say about you in your absence? This is a rare quality that most people look for when searching for potential friends or associates. If you want someone to like you, stand up for them in their absence. Your testimony about them to other people should be positive, one that will inspire their love for you.

You cannot possibly expect someone to like you if you speak negatively about them behind their back. Your words will haunt you should the one you intended for hears it. It should be something that you can confidently repeat to their face. Your sanctity will make you stand out when you stand up for your friends (pun intended).

Standing up for people you want to like you is a good way of 'shouting' your support for them. They will rush to see who it is that defended their character in public and will develop a special liking for you. Furthermore, you should do this in a manner that attracts respect and decorum to the one you are publicly defending.

4. Be Dignified

You are what you attract. It begins with your attributes and how you carry yourself around. This plays a significant role in the perception of other people towards you. What is their opinion about you? Is it desirable enough to make them like you? Work on how you present yourself to other people and you will be irresistibly likable.

There is never a second chance to make a first impression. It is up to you to ensure that the first impression which sticks is the correct one. Carry yourself with dignity in everything you do because you never know who is watching. Random strangers will automatically like you as they observe your personal and public life.

5. **Be Humble**

Humility is a rare virtue in most people. Nobody wants to be associated with violent friends because their rage makes them unpredictable. Humbleness does not mean you have allowed people to mistreat you. It means you are intelligent enough to choose your battles wisely.

Humble people are likable to a fault. People are attracted to calm personalities. They look mature, responsible, and chaos-free. Portray a positive image of yourself and you will be amazed at how people will like you.

Incorporating these five habits in your routine will make people like you and the icing of the cake is that whoever you aim to like you could be among them.

Chapter 7:
Happy People Reward Themselves

Do you ever wonder if the carrot and stick principle would still work in this world? The answer to this would be yes, the reward and punishment system still works, and you can always leverage it to build good habits. They, in turn, will help you reach your goal faster; that is why it is essential to celebrate your hard work and then afterward reward yourself for the effort you have been putting in. Gretchen Rubin, in her book Better than before, says,

"When we give ourselves treats, we feel energized, cared for, and contented, which boosts our self-command — and self-command helps us maintain our healthy habits."

If you do not get any rewards and treats, you will feel resentful angry, and you feel depleted. Imagine putting in all the hard work and then not getting anything in return. How would that make you feel? Bad, right? That is precisely why rewarding yourself is essential. We are going to outline 2 simple reasons why rewarding yourself is important.

1. **Reward makes you feel good and drives you further.**

How do you train pets, your dogs, and cats? You teach them with a treat. Just like them, our brain works the same way we can train ourselves to do a lot more work by rewarding ourselves. When you give yourself a treat, you will boost your mood, making you happy. When you give yourself a treat, your brain releases a chemical called dopamine that makes you feel good and happy. Even tho it is important to reward yourself, not all rewards give the same effect, and you should choose wisely so that those treats create positive reinforcement.

2. It works as positive reinforcement.

When a pleasant outcome follows your behavior, you are more likely to repeat the behavior. And this is called positive reinforcement. Connecting your hard work to rewards effectively not only gives you a mental break but also motivates you to want to do more of it. Therefore, use treats as positive reinforcement to build your momentum and grow your habits.

Just like this powerful saying from Tony Robbins:

"People who succeed have momentum. The more they succeed, the more they want to succeed, and the more they find a way to succeed. Similarly, when someone is failing, the tendency is to get on a downward spiral that can even become a self-fulfilling prophecy.

Happy People Have A Morning Ritual

For many of us, mornings begin in a rushed panic. We allow our alarm clocks to buzz at least a dozen times before deciding we have to get out of bed. Then we rush around our homes half-awake, trying to get ready for our day. In a hurry, we stub our toe on the bedpost, forget to put on deodorant, and don't pack a lunch because we simply don't have time. It's no wonder that so many folks despise the thought of being awake before 9 a.m.!

So it may not surprise you to know that the happiest and healthiest people tend to enjoy their mornings. They appear to thrive on waking up with the sun and look forward to a new day of possibilities. These people have humble morning rituals that increase their sense of well-being and give their day purpose.

Here are 3 morning habits that healthy and happy people tend to share:

1. **They wake up with a sense of gratitude**

Practicing gratitude is associated with a sense of overall happiness and a better mood—so it makes sense that the happiest and healthiest people we know start the day with a gratitude practice. This means that they're truly appreciative of their life and all of its little treasures. They practice small acts of gratitude in the morning by expressing thankfulness to their partner each morning before they rise from bed. They may also write about their gratefulness for five minutes each morning in a journal that they keep by their bedside.

2. **They begin every morning anew.**

The happiest and healthiest people know that every day is a brand-new day—a chance to start over and do something different. Yesterday may have been a complete failure for them, but today is a new day for success and adventure. Individuals who aren't ruined by one bad day are resilient creatures. <u>Resiliency</u> is a telltale sign of having purpose and happiness.

3. They take part in affirmation, meditation, or prayer.

Many of the happiest folks alive are <u>spiritual</u>. Affirmations are a way of reminding ourselves of all that we have going for us, and they allow us to engrain in our minds the kind of person we wish to be. <u>Meditation</u> helps keep our mind focused, calms our nerves, and supports inner peace. If you're already spiritual, prayer is a great way to connect and give thanks for whatever higher power you believe in.

Chapter 8:
Don't Stay At Home

Today we're going to talk about why you should consider getting out of your house as much as possible, especially if you need to get work done, or if you have some other important personal projects that requires your undivided attention to complete.

For those that work full-time jobs, we all aspire to one day be able to work from home. We all dream of one day being able to just get up from our beds and walk over to our desks to begin work.

Having tried this myself for the last 4 years, I can safely tell you that staying at home isn't all that amazing as it has been talked up or hyped up to be.

While it may sound nice to be able to work from home, in reality, distractions are tough to avoid, and procrastination is one major killer of productivity at home. Many of us have made our homes the Center of entertainment and relaxation. We buy nice couches, TVs, beds, speakers, etc, and all these items around the house are temptations for us to slack off.

For those who are living with family, or who have pets, their presence could also disrupt our productivity.

Without people around us to motivate us to keep working hard, we tend to just tell ourselves "it's okay I'll just watch this one show and then I'll get back to work", and before we know it, it is 5pm and we haven't done a single thing.

Some people love it, some people hate it, but personally, I much prefer getting my butt out of the house and into a co-working space, a cafe, or a library, where I can visually see other people working hard, which motivates me to stay away from slacking off.

Having been doing regular journaling to measure my productivity, staying at home has always resulted in my worst daily performance no matter how hard I try to make my home environment the most conducive for work. Feeling like taking nap because my bed is right there, or watching a Netflix show on my big screen tv, has always been hard to resist. You will be surprised how many hours you are potentially losing from just indulging in any of these things.

For those who really has no choice but to work from home, either to save money, or because you need to take care of a family member. I would highly suggest that you optimise your environment to give yourself the greatest chance of success.

Dedicate a room that will be made into your study/work room, ensure that there is adequate and bright lighting, and to Keep all possible distractions outside the room. Putting your work desk in your bedroom is the worst thing you can do because you will blur the lines between rest and work if you mix the two things up in one tiny space. Not only will you feel sluggish working from your bedroom, but you might also develop sleep issues as well.

Not staying at home is still your best bet for success. Find a space outside where you can be focused and have the discipline to get yourself there every single day, no matter how tired or lethargic you feel. Once you leave the house, you have already won half the battle in getting your productivity under control.

Happy People Are Optimistic

Beyond the simple reality that optimists are happier people (and happiness is what you're striving for), optimism has other benefits as well. So, if you want to achieve greater happiness, try being optimistic for a day.

Optimists enjoy a greater degree of academic success than pessimists do. Because optimistic students think it's possible for them to make a good grade, they study hardier and they study smarter. They manage the setting in which they study and they seek help from others when they need it. (Optimism, it turns out, is almost as predictive of how well students do in college as the SAT.)

Optimists are more self-confident than pessimists are. They believe in *themselves* more than fate.

Optimists are more likely to be problem-solvers than pessimists are. When pessimistic students get a D on a test, they tend to think things like: "I knew I shouldn't have taken this course. I'm no good at psychology." The optimistic student who gets a D says to herself, "I can do better. I just didn't study enough for this test. I'll do better next time." And she will.

Optimists welcome second chances after they fail more than pessimists do. Optimistic golfers always take a *mulligan* (a redo swing without penalty). Why? Because they expect to achieve a better result the second time around.

Optimists are more socially outgoing than pessimists are. Socially outgoing folks believe that the time they spend with other human beings makes them better in some way — smarter, more interesting, more attractive. Unfortunately, pessimists see little, if any, benefit from venturing out into the social world.

Optimists are not as lonely as pessimists are. Because pessimists don't see as much benefit from socializing with others, they have far fewer social and emotional connections in their lives, which is what loneliness is all about.

Optimists utilize social support more effectively than pessimists do. They aren't afraid to reach out in times of need.

Optimists are less likely to blame others for their misfortune than pessimists are. When you blame someone else for your troubles, what you're really saying is, "You're the *cause* of my problem and, therefore, you have to be the *solution* as well." Optimists have just as many troubles as pessimists throughout life — they just accept more responsibility for dealing with their misfortune.

Optimists cope with stress better than pessimists do. Pessimists worry, optimists act. A patient with coronary heart disease who is pessimistic "hopes and prays" that he doesn't have another heart attack anytime soon. The optimistic heart patient leaves little to chance — instead, he exercises regularly, practices his meditation exercises, adheres to a low-cholesterol diet, and makes sure he always gets a good night's sleep.

Chapter 9:
Happy People Spend Time Alone

No man is an island except for similarly as we blossom with human contact and connections, so too would we be able to prosper from time burned through alone. Also, this, maybe, turns out to be particularly important right now since we're all in detachment. We've since quite a while ago slandered the individuals who decide to be distant from everyone else, except isolation shouldn't be mistaken for forlornness. Here are two mental reasons why investing energy in isolation makes us more joyful and more satisfied:

1. **Spending time alone reconnects us.**

Our inclination for isolation might be transformative, as indicated by an examination distributed in the British Journal of Psychology in 2016. Utilizing what they call "the Savannah hypothesis of satisfaction," transformative clinicians Satoshi Kanazawa of the London School of Economics and Norman Li of Singapore Management University accept that the single, tracker accumulate way of life of our precursors structure the establishment of what satisfies us in present-day times. The group examined a study of 15,000 individuals matured somewhere between 18 and 28 in the United States. They found that individuals living in more thickly populated regions were fundamentally less cheerful than the individuals who lived in more modest networks.

"The higher the populace thickness of the prompt climate, the less glad" respondents were. The scientists accept this is because we had advanced mentally from when mankind, for the most part, existed on distant, open savannahs. Since quite a while ago, we have instilled an inclination to be content alone, albeit current life generally neutralizes that. Also, as good to beat all, they tracked down that the more clever an individual was, the more they appreciated investing energy alone. Along these lines, isolation makes you more joyful AND is evidence of your smarts. We're in.

2. Spending Time Alone Teaches Us Empathy

Investing in a specific measure of energy alone can create more compassion towards others than a milestone concentrate from Harvard. Scientists found that when enormous gatherings of individuals encircle us, it's harder for us to acquire viewpoints and tune into the sensations of others. However, when we venture outside that unique circumstance, the extra headspace implies we can feel for the situation of individuals around us in a more genuine and significant manner. Furthermore, that is uplifting news for others, but different investigations show that compassion and helping other people are significant to prosperity and individual satisfaction.

"At the point when you invest energy with a specific friend network or your colleagues, you foster a 'we versus them' attitude," clarifies psychotherapist and creator Amy Morin. "Investing energy alone assists you with growing more empathy for individuals who may not find a way into your 'inward circle.' "On the off chance that you're not used to isolation, it can feel awkward from the outset," she adds. "However, making that tranquil time for yourself could be critical to turning into the best form of yourself."

Chapter 10:
8 Ways On How To Start Taking Actions

Have you ever got caught up in situations when you can't bring yourself moving from deciding to doing? As a famous person once said, "Your beliefs become your thoughts; your thoughts become your words; your words become your actions; your actions become your habits; your habits become your values; your values become your destiny."

The first step towards success is by taking action. If you keep on thinking that you have to lose weight, start a business, learn a new language, or get another degree, you will end up nowhere without executing these thoughts into actions.

Here are 8 Ways To Start Moving The Needle In Your Life:

1. **Decide that you want to get out of your comfort zone**

The fear that we have that doesn't allow us to take action is that we might have to sacrifice our comfort zone in the process. And trust me, a lot of people aren't willing to do that. But if you don't step out of your comfort zone, how will you determine your true potential? You don't need the motivation to start taking action, and you just have to gather your willpower, stop with the excuses and procrastination, and get moving!

2. Don't indulge in the habit of Hesitatation

Have you had a great idea but then decide 10 minutes later that it was stupid. Ever wondered why that was? The answer is quite simple and straightforward; hesitation. We dwell on hesitation for too long. This makes it very difficult for us to get started on something. Thinking will only lead us to more and more thinking, which will lead us to a loop of continual thoughts, and our actions will get dominated by them. And then the regret that follows us is usually, "Why didn't we start earlier?" David Joseph Schwartz once said, "To fight fear, act. To increase fear – wait, put off, postpone."

3. Stop waiting for the perfect time:

There's a Chinese proverb that says, "The best time to plant a tree was 20 years ago. The second-best time is now." It means that there is no such thing as perfect timing. The minute we start to take action, the time becomes perfect. If we wait till everything gets in order or becomes exemplary, then we will be waiting forever. The ideal time in your eyes was last year, but the second-best time is right here and right now. It's never too late to start with your goals, dreams, and passions. All we have in our hands is the present time and what counts is how efficiently we spend this time. We must take action now and make adjustments along the way if we feel like it.

4. Don't pause and wait:

Have you ever found yourself thinking that, hey, it's a good day to wander around the city, but found yourself sitting and wasting time watching TV? Or you thought of doing your assignment but got caught up in a more hopeless task? Or you thought of presenting a new idea to your boss but got shied away? All of these thoughts, no matter how positive they were, stand nowhere unless you implement them. So stop being a talker and start being a doer. A doer is someone who immediately moves forward with his ideas. When we pause and look around, we will find ourselves making excuses and allow doubts to creep through into our minds. "The most difficult thing is the decision to act; the rest is merely tenacity." - Amelia Earhart.

5. Stop Over-thinking:

There's always an endless loop of overthinking that we can't get over with no matter how hard we try. From imagining the worst-case scenarios of even the best situations to getting anxious and depressed whenever any minor inconvenience happens, our mind tricks us into thinking that we can never get the best of both worlds (HM fans, I gotcha!) When we overthink stuff, we tend to get paralysis of analysis. We start to analyze every situation and obsess over how things aren't perfect, or the conditions aren't going our way. We question the amount of time that we have to commit and make endless excuses and reasons not to move forward with whatever we want to do.

6. Take continuous action:

The first step is the hardest step that we have to take. But once you get started, make sure that you fully commit yourself to your goal. Take continuous actions and keep up with your momentum by doing something related to your plan every day. Even if you are scheduling only 15-20 minutes of your life completing a small task, it will eventually add up into the more remarkable things. Moreover, it will help you build confidence by seeing your achievements. "It does not matter how slowly you go as long as you do not stop." - Confucius.

7. **Overcome your fears:**

We often succumb to our fears before even taking a step. The fear of failure, of not being good enough, of not doing enough, is the most common among them. Our mind tricks us into thinking that we might end up failing sooner or later. This prevents us from taking the first step and implementing our thoughts into actions. For example, suppose you're a professional speaker at a public speaking event. You have gained loads of experience, and you have no problem speaking to the lobby. But you do feel yourself getting nervous when you have to wait around for your turn. However, once you get started, all that fear and anxiety disappear. If you face similar situations in life, start being a doer, take action towards it and see how it will boost your confidence.

8. **Eliminate any distractions:**

We live in a world where distractions and procrastination have become more important than productivity. Have you ever found yourself thinking that you will take the online lecture for the subject you have been struggling with but ended up checking your social media accounts or watching irrelevant videos on YouTube? Procrastination is the primary reason we never end up doing what we should keep in our priorities. Instead, we should focus on our tasks, eliminate all the distractions and start with a slow but steady pace towards our goal. A single average idea put into action is far more valuable than those 20 genius ideas saved for another day or another time.

Conclusion:

Achieving your goals and dreams isn't an overnight task but takes years and decades to give you the final fruits. It's a road that will have setbacks, obstacles, lessons, and challenges. But what matters is that we shouldn't give up. We should face all the struggles and not surrender ourselves to our fears and demotivation. Converting your thoughts into actions and then enjoying the journey will equip you to thrive and see your goals become a reality in no time. So take into account what steps you took today. No matter how small they may be, appreciate and celebrate them.

PART 3

Chapter 1:
7 Ways To Attract Happiness

We have seen a lot of people defining success as to their best of knowledge. While happiness is subjective from person to person, there's a law of attraction that remains constant for everyone in the world. It states that you will indirectly start to attract all the good things in life when you become happier. This is why happy people often have good lives where everything just somehow tends to work for them. Happiness not only feels good but can also make our manifestation attempts twice as effective. We shouldn't measure our happiness from external factors but instead, as cliche as it may sound, we should know that true happiness comes from the inside.

Here are some ways for you to attract happiness:

1. **Make a choice to be happy:**

When you choose to be as happy as you can in every moment of your life, your subconscious mind will start acknowledging your decision, and it will begin to find ways to bring more joy into your life. When you work towards your decision of being happy, the universe also plays its part and makes sure it attracts more situations in your life that you can be pleased about. The positive vibrations that you will give out will find their way back to you. You don't have to make the decision of being happy right away, as some of you might be going through a tough time. Sit, relax, and take some time to reflect on yourself first and then make a choice whenever you're ready.

2. Define What Happiness Means To You

We have also found ourselves asking this question a million times, "what exactly is happiness?" Some people would attach the idea of happiness with materialistic things such as a big house, expensive cars, branded clothes and shoes, designer bags, the latest technologies, and so forth. While for some, happiness is merely spending time with family and friends, doing the things that they love, and finding inner peace and calm.

3. React Positively under all situations:

We could experience a thousand good things but a million bad ones in our everyday lives. And sometimes, it could be complicated for us to encounter any kind of happiness given the circumstances. Although these circumstances cannot be in our control, how we react to them is always in our hands. As our favorite Professor Dumbledore once said, "Happiness can be found even in the darkest of times if only one remembers to turn on the light." Similarly, we should always try to find that silver lining at the end of the dark tunnel, always seek some positivity in every situation. But we are only humans. Don't try to enforce positivity on yourself if you don't feel like it. It's okay to address all our emotions equally till you be yourself again.

4. Do not procrastinate:

You might find it a bit weird, but procrastination does snatch your happiness away. No matter how much things are going well in your life, you would always find a loophole, a reason to be unhappy and dissatisfy with yourself a well as your life. Procrastination makes you believe that you are not living up to your fullest potential. You will get this nagging feeling that will eventually morph into negative emotions that would nearly eat you. So, try to avoid procrastination as much as possible and start doing the things that actually matter.

5. **Stay present:**

The key to becoming more focused, more at peace, more effective in manifesting, and eventually, much happier is to just live in the moment. Whatever you're doing in the present, try to be completely aware and focused on it. It will help you avoid all the negative feelings you have conjured up about the past and future. Try to stay present as much as you can; over time, it will become a habit, and you will develop the capability to face it all. This will definitely help you attract more happiness into your life.

6. **Do not compare yourself:**

As Theodore Rosevelt once said, "Comparison is the thief of joy." Whenever we compare ourselves to others, we tend to become ungrateful and strip ourselves of the ability to appreciate the good and abundance in our lives. We start to magnify the good in other people's lives and the bad that is in our own. We must understand that everyone is going through their own pace, and they all are secretly struggling with one thing or the other.

7. **Don't try too hard:**

Happiness demands patience. It is better to get into it gradually rather than being overeager. Many people take the law of attraction and being positive a little too far and start obsessing over it. They tend to panic if they get negative thoughts or are unable to attract the things they want. Don't get frustrated if things don't work out your way, and don't give up on the idea of happiness if you feel distressed. Try to prioritize your happiness and give others a reason to be happy too. Make yours as well as other's lives easy.

Conclusion:

Not many people know that, but being happy is actually the foundation towards attracting all your dreams and goals. When you adopt the habit of becoming truly happy every day, everything good will naturally follow you. Over time, happiness can even become your default state. Try your best to follow the guidelines above, and I guarantee that you will start feeling happier immediately.

Chapter 2:
Happy People Plan Their Week in Advance for Maximum Productivity

There you are, enjoying a perfectly beautiful Sunday evening. You've had an eventful and fun weekend and decided to spend tonight chillaxing. Then, from out of nowhere, a sense of dread washes over you (there arose such a clatter?). Your mind begins to think about what you need to get done this week. There's just no way to stop these thoughts once they get rolling.

But, how exactly should you plan your week so that it will be more productive? Well, here are two tips that will guarantee that your week will be efficient and effective.

1. **Get a head start**

"Sunday clears away the rust of the whole week." — Joseph Addison

It's true. If you want to have a productive week, then you need to start planning on Sundays. If that's not your cup of tea, though, then at least begin your preparations on Friday afternoon or Saturday.

I know. You want to kick back and relax this weekend. But, is it going to be the end of the world if you do a little work? Could you map out your week while watching football or waiting for your favorite HBO to start?

Set aside about an hour and jot down everything you need to get done this week. In particular, think about your daily routines, recurring events, deadlines, and goals. Next, mark them off first so that nothing else gets scheduled ahead of them. Don't forget about anything else that you've penciled in. Remember you are going to that concert with a friend or your family coming to town?

That may sound like a lot of work. But, it gets all of these commitments out of your head. From there, you can begin to plan accordingly. For example, because you have family arriving on Thursday, you'll probably want to make sure that you get your most important work done in advance so that you can spend time with them.

2. **Use the E/N/D system.**

The E/N/D system, which stands for Energizing / Neutral / Draining, can be used to help [you prioritize](#) your time. It accomplishes this by [helping you manage your energy](#).
Whenever scheduling tasks, designate them as either E, N, or D. Usually, energizing tasks are the things you enjoy doing. As such, you would want to schedule them when you need an energy boost, like after lunch. Draining tasks are those that you dread because they're challenging. Those should be scheduled when you have the most energy, like in the morning.

Chapter 3:
5 Scientific Tricks To Become Perfectly Happy

Being happy comes naturally. Almost everything around us makes us happy in a certain way. Being happy is a constant feeling inside a human being. They always tend to get satisfied, even at a minimum. Everywhere we look nowadays, we see things filled with this bright emotion. We tune to the songs written about happiness, we see posters at every corner about being happy, and most importantly, we have people who make us happy. Being happy comes freely, without any fee.
There are scientific ways to become happy because an average human is always looking for more.

Some ways in which you'll feel full at heart and eased at mind. A burst of good laughter is like medicine to the core. So, science has given us ways to take this medicine without and cautions. Being happy is one of the least harmful emotions. It binds people together. Even some forms have been scientifically proven to work in favor of our happiness. There is almost no end to those bright smiles on our lips or those crinkles by our eyes. As it said, smiling is contagious. And we all prefer to smile back at everyone who smiles at us automatically. Here are some scientific ways to be happy.

1. **Minutes Into Exercise**

It is proven that some exercise helps you to smile and laugh more. If there is an exercise to be happy with, then people would be sure to give it a try now and then. Exercise helps us to regulate our jaw muscle, so it will be easier to pass a smile next time. There is also meditation. It enables you to calm your mind and leads towards an easier life. It usually helps to keep you at peace so you'll feel happier towards the things that should make you happy. You'll start to get more content at certain or small items. It becomes a habit slowly to smile more, be more satisfied. Being happy also benefits others, and then they will be more inclined to be pleased towards you.

2. **Get Enough Sleep**

Another scientifically proven way to get happy is to sleep enough every night. It helps with the formation of a proper mindset towards your happiness in life. Sleeping at least 8 hours a day is a must for being happy; if not, the 7 hours would suffice enough for you to smile a little more. It keeps your mind and soul at a steady pace, which is inclined to keep us calm and collected. Keeping calm and organized is one of the factors to be happy. Wake up early to listen to the birds or go for a morning run. Keep yourself fresh in the morning to be a better and happier person.

Early to bed is a wise men choice. So, get a sound slumber every night to have a sunny morning following you.

3. Take A Break Now and Then

Even the greatest minds need some rest, so it's only average for a human to get some rest after a long period of working day and night. Go on a vacation. Get a leave because life needs to be enjoyed through anything. Working all the time makes you dull and unhappy. So, make sure to take a break once in a while to start again with a fresh mind and perform a better duty. Don't load yourself with the things that won't matter in a few years. Take vacation so you'll have a more peaceful time ahead of you in your life.

4. Build Your Happy Place

People tend to get tired quickly and often by working all the time. All most of the time, vacation can't seem like an option. So, the best place to visit in such a situation is your happy place—a place you have created in your mind where you are so glad all the time. Just by imagining such a place, you get comfortable and tend to keep working and being pleased with the same time. Your happy place gives you joy, and you become a happier person overall. And it is just easier to carry your vacation with you all the time.

5. Count Your Achievements

A great way to be scientifically happy is to count all the achievements you have made so far. Even count little things like watering plants as an achievement because it gives you a sense of joy. Achievements tell you that you have done more in your life than you intended to, and you will get motivated to do more every time. It makes you believe in yourself and get you going only forwards. You get happy with the deeds you have done till now, and it helps you plan your next good achievement. You naturally become more inclined to fulfill your desires and needs. All the things you have done so far will make you feel beneficial to society and happier for yourself.

Conclusion

Being happy is a great feeling with a more remarkable result in life. So, smiling more won't do you any wrong; in fact, it may be good for you to stretch your jaw a little. Happiness doesn't discriminate, so it will be good to spread this scientific happiness as much as we can. Being happy gives us a sense of undeniable joy and a vision of a positive and bright future.

Chapter 4:
Happy People Focus on What They Are Good at

Steve Jobs said, "Your work is going to fill a large part of your life, and the only way to be truly satisfied is to do what you believe is great work. And the only way to do great work is to love what you do." Your family and society put a lot of pressure on you for being a specific type of successful usually. That falls under the false lines of what society considers successful: being socially important and having a lot of wealth. Still, when you focus on money and superficial status, you will not be able to live a truly fulfilling life. Even when in your office you focus on tasks that you find difficult or displeasing, you will feel frustrated. Now, I quoted Steve Jobs in the start that man is a huge example for all of us; he focused on what he liked and eventually became successful.

You do not have to stray from your talents. If you enjoy doing something and it comes easily to you, there are high chances of being a leader in that field because you are naturally good at it. There is always the pressure of achieving what other people consider success, and you have to resist it. When you focus on things you are good at, you have to realize that when you focus on things you are good at, you do not have to try too hard things will eventually fall into place. That certainly does not mean that you never have to try new things. You should always take new opportunities because you can find things you are good at.

To know that you are good at something is another thing and to be modest about it is another. If you think someone would be interested in what you are good at, tell them. Let people know your skills because if there is a project or job prospect, people will know who they need to contact. Secondly, you can never be great at everything, so you should narrow your field of expertise and then practice those. That will help you grow. Plus, in your workplace, you do not need to shy away from new opportunities. If there are tasks, you think you are good at, volunteer for them. This way, your superiors will also get to know about your skills and interests, and you never know what they might have in store for you.

You need to be self-aware; if you think you are good at something, you probably because you will meet many people in life that will try to side-track you. They will tell you that people are not interested in what you are trying to sell or wasting your time and should do what everyone else is doing. Every person you meet will have an opinion of their own, but you need to remember you are the only one that has control over their life, so you do not need to be intimidated into thinking that what you are good at is not worth it.

Happy People Choose to Exercise

There is a feeling you get when you just finish your workout, and you feel amazing, much better than you were feeling before. Even when you are not feeling motivated to go to the gym, just thinking about this feeling makes you get up, leave your bed and get going to the gym. This feeling can also be called an endorphin rush. Exercise indeed makes you happier in multiple ways.

Firstly, movement helps you bond with others that are in the brain chemistry of it all. Your heart rate is going up, you are using your body, engaging your muscles, your brain chemistry will change, and it will make it easier for you to connect and bond with other people. It also changes how your trust people. Research also showed that social pressures like a hug, laughing, or high-five are also enhanced. You will also find your new fitness fam, the people you will be working out with, and because you will have a shared interest that is having a healthy lifestyle will help you have a stronger bond with them. And as experts say that having strong relationships and connections in life will help you in overall happiness.

We have already discussed those exercise increases endorphins but what you do not know is that it increases a lot more brain chemicals that make you feel happy and good about yourself. Some of the brain chemicals that increase are; dopamine, endorphins, endocannabinoid and adrenaline. All of these chemicals are associated with feeling confident, capable, and happy. The amount of stress, physical pain, and anxiety also decrease significantly. A chemical that your body creates when your muscles contract is called "myokine", it is also shown to boost happiness and relieve stress.

Secondly, exercise can help boost your confidence, and of course, when it comes to feeling empowered and happy, confidence is the key. "At the point when you move with others, it's anything but a solid feeling of 'greater than self' probability that causes individuals to feel more idealistic and enabled, "Also, it permits individuals to feel more engaged turning around the difficulties in their own lives. What's more, that is a fascinating side advantage of moving with others because there's an encapsulated feeling of 'we're in the same boat' that converts into self-assurance and the capacity to take on difficulties in your day; to day existence."

Thirdly, exercising outdoors affects your brain, similar to meditation. In case you're similar to the innumerable other people who have found out about the advantages of contemplation yet can't make the time, uplifting news. You may not need to contemplate to get a portion of the advantages. Researchers found that exercising outside can similarly affect the cerebrum and disposition as reflection. Exercising outside immediately affects a state of mind that is amazingly incredible for wretchedness and nervousness. Since it's anything but a state in your mind that is the same as contemplation, the condition of open mindfulness,"

Chapter 5:
7 Ways On How To Attract Success In Life

Successful people fail more times than unsuccessful people try. A new thought author and metaphysical writer Florence Scovel Shinn in her timeless 1940 novel, 'the secret door to success,' suggests that "Success is not a secret, it is a system." Throughout the centuries, the leaders have alluded to the possibility that success can be attracted into one's life simply by thinking and doing. It is rather a planned journey as we give validity to the premise of creating a plan or setting a goal for ourselves. Goals are set to be achieved, and achievements pave the way for success. Here are 7 Ways To Attract Success In Your Life:

1. Define What Success Means To You

Success is subjective to the person who seeks to obtain it, and the ideas may be different for each other. For some of us, success means wealth. For some, it means health and happiness. While for some, it is the mere effort of getting out of bed every day. But the thing that is most highlighted is that we can never get success without struggling. Every one of us wants success, but we do not know how to bring about that life-changing phenomenon that will take us to the zenith of our potential.

2. Begin with Gratitude:

From flying to the sky to crashing to the ground, be always thankful to wherever life takes you. Always start by being grateful for what you already have. Whether it's good or bad, we cannot climb the stairs of success without having experiences. If we make mistakes, we should make sure not to give up, rather learn from those mistakes. We must strive to embrace our flaws and imperfections. If we tend to fall seven times, we must have the energy to get up eight times. Whatever life throws us at, no matter the obstacles and challenges, we should always be in a state of gratitude and always be thankful for our learning.

3. Stop making excuses:

Your decisions lead to your destiny. If you are thinking about delaying your work or 'chilling' first, then someone else will take that opportunity for himself. You either grab on the opportunities from both hands, or you sit on the sidelines and watch someone else steal your spotlight. There's no concept of resting and being lazy when you have to work towards your goals and achieve your dreams. One of the major mistakes of unsuccessful people is that they make endless excuses. They would avoid their tasks in any way instead of working on them and actually doing them. You will attract success only if you put your mind towards something and work hard towards it.

4. Realize your potential:

The fine line between incredibly hardworking people and yet fail to achieve success, and the ones who are at the peak of their respective field is simple – potential. We never realize our true potential until we are put in a situation where there's no way out but to express our abilities. We might think that people have more excellent skills than us or have more knowledge than us. But the truth is, we have more potential inside of us. This might be tougher to implement as we don't know how well we can handle things while stressing out or how much hidden talents and skills we possess. Our potential is merely what might make us successful or a failure. It all depends on how much we are willing to try and push ourselves forward.

5. Celebrate the success of others:

What you wish upon others finds its way and comes back to you again. While seeing people being successful in their professional and personal lives and making a fortune in their careers and businesses can be tough on our lives, always remember that they too faced struggles and challenges before reaching here. There's no need to be envious as life has an abundance of everything to offer to everyone. Whatever is it in your destiny will always find its way to you. You can't snatch what others have achieved, and similarly, others can't seize whatever that you have or may achieve. Congratulate people around you and be excited for them. Send out positive vibes to everyone so you may receive the same.

6. Behave as if you are successful:

Have you heard of the term "fake it till you make it?" Well, it applies to this scenario too. You can fake your success and act like a successful person until you really become one. First, surround yourself with lucrative people. See what habits they have developed over time, how they dress up, how they behave, and, most importantly, how much work they do daily to achieve their goals. Get inspired from them and adopt their healthy habits. Be successful in your own eyes first so that eventually you can be successful in other's eyes as well.

7. Provide value for others:

While money and fame are the most common success goals, we should first try to focus on creating value in the world. A lot of successful people wanted to change things in the world first and help people out. Mark Zuckerberg built a tool for Harvard students initially and now has over 1.4 billion users. The first thing on our mind after waking up shouldn't be money or success, and it would be to create value for the world and the people around us.

Conclusion:

It would be best if you strived to explore the unique, endless possibilities within you. Then, when you start working on yourself, you're adding to your mind's youth, vitality, and beauty.

Chapter 6:

Constraints Make You Better: Why the Right Limitations Boost Performance

It is not uncommon to complain about the constraints in your life. Some people say that they have little time, money, and resources, or their network is limited. Yes, some of these things can hold us back, but there is a positive side to all of this. These constraints are what forces us to make choices and cultivate talents that can otherwise go undeveloped. Constraints are what drives creativity and foster skill development. In many ways reaching the next level of performance is simply a matter of choosing the right constraints.

How to Choose the Right Constraints

There are three primary steps that you can follow when you are using constraints to improve your skills.

1. **Decide what specific skill you want to develop.**

The more specific you are in the skill, the easier it will be to design a good constraint for yourself. You shouldn't try to develop the skill of being "good at marketing," for example. It's too broad. Instead, focus on learning how to write compelling headlines or analyze website data—something specific and tangible.

2. **Design a constraint that requires this specific skill to be used**

There are three main options for designing a constraint: time, resources, and environment.

- **Time:** Give yourself less time to accomplish a task or set a schedule that forces you to work on skills more consistently.

- **Resources:** Give yourself fewer resources (or different resources) to do a task.

- **Environment:** According to one study, if you eat on 10-inch plates rather than 12-inch plates, you'll consume 22 percent fewer calories over a year. One simple change in the environment can lead to significant results. In my opinion, environmental constraints are best because they impact your behavior without you realizing it.

3. **Play the game**

Constraints can accelerate skill development, but they aren't a magic pill. You still need to put in your time. The best plan is useless without repeated action. What matters most is getting your reps in.

The idea is to practice, experiment with different constraints to boost your skills. As for myself, I am working on storytelling skills these days. I have some friends who are amazing storytellers. I've never been great at it, but I'd like to get better. The constraint I've placed on myself is scheduling talks without the use of slides. My last five speaking engagements have used no slides or a few basic images. Without text to rely on, I have designed a constraint that forces me to tell better stories so that I don't embarrass myself in front of the audience.

So, the question here is What do you want to become great at? What skills do you want to develop? Most importantly, what constraints can you place upon yourself to get there? Figure these things out and start from today!

10 Habits of Bernard Arnault

Bernard Arnault- French investor, businessman, and CEO of LVMH recently reclaimed the title "worlds' wealthiest" from fellow billionaire Jeff Bezos. His business acumen and awe-inspiring financial achievements deserve to be recognized. His perspective can serve as a model for entrepreneurs who want to follow in his footsteps.

Bernard Arnault has written about money, prosperity, leadership, and power over the years. Moreover, his path to becoming the CEO of one of the world's most recognized brands will provide you with valuable lessons to emulate from. That is, your life circumstances shouldn't stop you from expanding and thriving outside your expertise.

Following his impressive accomplishments, here are ten points you can take away from Arnault's journey to success.

1. **Happiness Before Money**

According to Bernard, happiness is leading. That is leading your team to the top whether you are in business, sports, music industry. Money, according to him, is a consequence, and success is a blend of your past and future.

Your priority is not what you'll make sooner! When you put much-required effort into your job, profits will flow.

2. **Mistakes Your Lesson**

Your biggest mistake is your learning opportunity. When your business isn't performing well, understand the situation first and be patient.

In the world of innovative brands, it can take years to get something to work. Give it time and put yourself in a long-term expectation.

3. Always Behave as a Startup

Think small. Act quickly. Smaller boats can turn faster than more giant tankers. Arnault emphasizes the significance of thinking small. LVMH, in Arnault's opinion, is not a massive corporation device with miles of unnecessary bureaucracy.

Believe in your vision while attracting the best talent for your success path. A handy, adaptable speed, one that can fail quickly as easy to sleeve up.

4. Continuously Reinvent Yourself

How do you maintain your relevance? Bernard's LVMH is built on innovation, quality, entrepreneurship, and, essentially, on long-term vision. LVMH excels at developing increasingly desirable new products and selling them globally.

To be successful today, with your capabilities, opt for a worldwide startup and see what's going on. This necessitates a more considerable investment, which gives you an advantage. However, let the Creators run your inventions.

5. Team-Creative Control

Arnault strategies find creative control under each product's team to do what they do best. Arnault's designers are the dreamer's realists and critics. Allow your team to take creative control. You risk putting a tourniquet around their minds if you restrict them in any way.

6. **Create Value To Attract Customers**

Marketing investigates what the customer desires. As a result, you are doing what they need: creating a product and testing it to see if it works. Keeping your products in close contact with consumers, according to Arnault, makes a desire to buy in them. LVMH creates products that generate customers. For him, it's never about sales; it's always about creating desire. Your goal should be to be desirable for long-term marketability.

7. **Trust the Process**

There will always be different voices in business, and while there will undoubtedly be good advice, if you believe an idea will succeed, you may need to persevere until the end. Like Arnault, disregard your critics by following through with your vision to excel.

8. **Your Persistence Is Everything**

It would be best if you were very persistent. It would be best to have ideas, but the idea is only 20% of the equation. The execution rate is 80%. So if you are trying out a startup, having ideas marvellous, the driving force is persistence and execution.

When it comes to the most successful startups, such as Facebook, the idea was great from the beginning. Others, however, had the same idea. So why is Facebook such a phenomenal success today? It is critically through execution with persistence.

9. Do Not Think of Yourself

Bernard Arnault can be differentiated from other billionaires like Elon Musk or Bill Gates by focusing on the brands, making their longevity rather than making himself the face. He is only concerned with promoting his products.

To accomplish this, you must maintain contact with pioneers and designers, for example, while also making their ideas more specific and sustainable.

10. Maintain Contact With Your Company

One of the most common leadership mistakes is to lose sight of the company once you reach the top and "stick" with manageable goals. Instead, to see if the machine is working correctly or if there is room for improvement, you must examine every corner and every part of it.

Conclusion

Your willingness to outwork and your ability to outlearn everyone will keep your success journey intact and going. Bernard Arnault's path to becoming the CEO of the worlds most recognized and desired multibillion empire of brands have a valuable lesson for you: your starting point does not influence or determine your future destination.

Chapter 7:
Happy People Only Focus on What Is Within Their Control

We cloud our judgment and lose the sense of our role in shaping our reality.

Such can be the case today.

We're fighting through a global pandemic, and I can assure you every one of us is having good days and bad days.

On the good days, we try to stay positive and be productive. On the bad days, we sulk into the worry of predicting what the future will be like. We imagine it, and then we start living it, which leaves us feeling helpless and scared.

Thoughts fire before emotions—that's why when we think negatively, we feel negative emotions.

But there's a way around this.

Whenever I find myself moving from a positive outlook to a negative one, I try my best to bring my attention back to the most important aspect of all.

I ask myself these three questions:

1. What is worrying me?
2. What is within my control?
3. What matters most to me, and what can I do about it?

When we focus on what we can control, our thoughts empower us and then trigger positive emotions.

Do we give our power away to factors we cannot control, or do we retain it and direct our energy onto the options we can control?

When my mind plays tricks on me and slides me into a stream of worry, I consciously try to swim out of it. And I use this framework below to reorient my thoughts and whisk them up into a more sunny state of mind.

A Sunshine State of Mind

At any given stage in your life, regardless of the set of circumstances you are dealing with, you can find yourself in one of four mental states:

- **Quadrant #1: Wasting your energy.** When you focus on what is not within your control, you're wasting your energy on factors that will not move you forward. This is like having a 2-week vacation booked, which was canceled due to the pandemic. You can complain all you want, but what's the use? Stop draining your energy on it and start thinking clearly.

- **Quadrant #2: Being paranoid.** When you ignore what is not within your control, you're paranoid. You shouldn't ignore external factors, instead, accept what is and be aware of the external conditions that are outside your control. For instance, with this pandemic, we must understand the situation and how it progresses because its advancements have implications on our lives. We don't want to give our undivided attention, but we do want to stay educated on it.

- **Quadrant #3: In a sunshine state of mind.** When you focus on what is within your control, you're in the driver's seat. You're intentional about your attitude and how you spend your energy. This is where you are emotionally mature and thinking rationally and clearly in a sunshine state of mind. And what does it do to you? It keeps you positive, energized, and motivated.

Happy People Don't Hold on To Grudges

Holding a grudge is when you harbor anger, bitterness, resentment, or other negative feelings long after someone has done something to hurt you. Usually, it's in response to something that's already occurred. Other times a grudge may develop after simply perceiving that someone is against you or means you harm—whether or not they do. Grudges also often feature persistent rumination about the person and/or incident at the center of your ill-will.

While we don't often like to admit it, holding a grudge is a common way some people respond to the feeling that they've been wronged. If you're still mad well after a precipitating incident, you may be holding on to those negative feelings for too long, sometimes well after other people typically would have let them go. You may remember multiple past bad acts and relive those experiences every time you think about or interact with that person—either making your displeasure abundantly clear to them or keeping your true feelings to yourself. You might be intentionally holding a grudge, but sometimes you aren't even aware of it.

But whatever your intentions or the cause of your bitterness, holding a grudge can end up hurting you as much as the person who inspired it. Learn more about how clinging to anger can impact you emotionally, physically, and socially, as well as how to begin to let go of your grudges and cope with anger more healthily. From early childhood on, holding a grudge is one-way people respond to negative feelings and events. This reaction is particularly common when you think someone has done something intentionally, callously, or thoughtlessly to hurt you, especially if they don't seem to care or make an attempt to apologize or make the situation right.

If you have low self-esteem, poor coping skills, were embarrassed by the hurt, and/or have a short temper, you may be even more likely to hold a grudge. While we all may fall into holding an occasional grudge, some people may be more prone to hanging on to resentments or anger than other people. Sometimes, holding grudges—and blaming others—may be a form of self-protection. In the same vein, some people may be more conscious that they are stoking feelings of bitterness than others, which may be unaware of their role in keeping their anger alive. Lasting bitterness can grow from a variety of issues—large and small—as well.

Chapter 8:
Happy People Are Busy but Not Rushed

Dan Pink points to an interesting new research finding — the happiest people are those that are very busy but don't feel rushed:

Who among us are the happiest? Newly published research suggests that fortunate folks have little or no excess time and yet seldom feel rushed.

This clicks with me. I love blogging, but I hate being under time pressure to get it done. This tension is very nicely demonstrated in a recent study by Hsee et al. (2010). When given a choice, participants preferred to do nothing unless given the tiniest possible reason to do something: a piece of candy. Then they sprang into action.

Not only did people only need the smallest inducement to keep busy, but they were also happier when doing something rather than nothing. It's as if people understand that being busy will keep them happier, but they need an excuse of some kind.

Having plenty of time gives you a feeling of control. Anything that increases your *perception of control* over a situation (whether it increases your control or not) can substantially decrease your stress level.

In Colorado, Steve Maier at the University of Boulder says that the degree of control that organisms can exert over something that creates stress determines whether the stressor alters the organism's functioning. His findings indicate that only uncontrollable stressors cause harmful effects. Inescapable or uncontrollable stress can be destructive, whereas the same stress that feels escapable is less destructive, significantly so… **Over and over, scientists see that the perception of control over a stressor alters the stressor's impact.**

But heavy time pressure stresses you out and kills creativity. Low-to-moderate time pressure produces the best results.

If managers regularly set impossibly short time-frames or impossibly high workloads, employees become stressed, unhappy, and unmotivated—burned out. Yet, people hate being bored. It was rare for any participant in our study to report a day with very low time pressure, such days—when they did occur—were also not conducive to positive inner work life. In general, low-to-moderate time pressure seems optimal for sustaining positive thoughts, feelings, and drives.

Your reaction to being too busy and under time pressure might be to want to do nothing. But that can drop you into the bottom left corner. And this makes you more unhappy than anything:

…**surveys "continue to show the least happy group to be those who quite often have excess time." Boredom, it seems, is burdensome.**

So, stay busy—set goals. Challenge yourself, but make sure you have plenty of time to feel in control of the situation.

This is how games feel. And games are fun.

Chapter 9:
Being 100% Happy Is Overrated

Lately I've been feeling as though happiness isn't something that truly lasts. Happiness isn't something that will stay with us very long. We may feel happy when we are hanging out with friends, but that feeling will eventually end once we part for the day. I've been feeling as though expecting to be constantly happy is very overrated. We try to chase this idea of being happy. We chase the material possessions, we chase the fancy cars, house, and whatever other stuff that we think will make us happy. But more often than not the desire is never really fulfilled. Instead, i believe that the feeling accomplishment is a much better state of mind to work towards. Things will never make us happy. We may enjoy the product we have worked so hard for temporarily. But that feeling soon goes away. And we are left wondering what is the next best thing we can aim our sights on. This never-ending chase becomes a repetitive cycle, one that we never truly are aware of but constantly desire. We fall into the trap that finding happiness is the end all-be-all.

What i've come to realise is that most of the time, we are actually operating on a more baseline level. A state that is skewed more towards the neutral end. Neither truly happy, or neither truly sad. And I believe that is perfectly okay. We should allow ourselves to embrace and accept the fact that it is okay to be just fine. Just neutral. Sure it isn't something very exciting, but we shouldn't put ourselves in a place where we expect to be constantly happy in order to lead a successful life. This revelation came when I realised that every time I felt happy, I would experience a crash in mood the next day.

Happy Who? Happy You!

I would start looking at instagram, checking up on my friends, comparing their days, and thinking that they are leading a happier life than I was. I would then start berating myself and find ways to re-create those happy moments just for the sake of it. Just because I thought i needed to feel happy all the time. It was only when I actually sat down and started looking inwards did I realise that maybe I can never truly find happiness from external sources.

Instead of trying to find happiness in things and external factors that are beyond my control, I started looking for happiness from within myself. I began to appreciate how happy I was simply being alone. Being by myself. Not letting other factors pull me down. I found that I was actually happiest when I was taking a long shower, listening to my own thoughts. No music playing, no talking to people, just me typing away on my computer, writing down all the feelings I am feeling, all the thoughts that I am thinking, letting every emotion I was feeling out of my system. I started to realise that the lack of distractions, noise, comparisons with others, free from social media, actually provided me with a clearer mind. It was in those brief moments where I found myself to be my most productive, with ideas streaming all over the place. It was in that state of mind that I did feel somewhat happy. That I could create that state of mind without depending on other people to fulfil it for me.

If any of you out there feel that your emotions are all over the place, maybe it is time for you to sit down by yourself for a little while. Stop searching for happiness in things and stuff, and sometimes even people. We think it is another person's job to make us happy. We expect to receive compliments, flowers, a kiss, in order to feel happy. While those things are certainly nice to have, being able to find happiness from within is much better. By sitting and reflecting in a quiet space, free from any noise and distractions, we may soon realise that maybe we are okay being just okay. Maybe we don't need expensive jewellery or handbags or fancy houses to make us happy. Maybe we just need a quiet mind and a grateful spirit.

The goal is to find inner peace. To accept life for the way it is. To accept things as the way they are. To be grateful for the things we have. That is what it means to be happy.

"Happy People Enjoy the Hidden Pleasures life has to offer."

It is said that the best things in your life are free, and there is not even a shred of doubt in that life is filled with satisfying hidden pleasures. To feel fulfilled, you need to enjoy them, so we are going to list some of the most simple, satisfying hidden pleasures life has to offer so that next time when you find yourself in a similar situation, you take out a moment and truly enjoy it:

Finding money you did not know you had: Reaching into your pocket and finding out a dollar 20 bill from the last time you went out wearing those jeans brings absolute joy all of a sudden. You have some extra money on you that you completely forgot about.

Receiving a Real letter via snail mail: Since email is more used these days, it has become the primary source of written communication, and most of the things you find in your snail mail are junk. So, when you find a package or a letter from someone you know in the mail, it brings joy, and a sense of excitement takes over you as you start opening the gift.

Making Brief Eye Contact with Someone of the Opposite Sex: We are all so busy in our lives, and most of the times when we are out, we spend time looking at our screens, so sometimes there is a rare moment where you pass them in a subway or street, and they look at you momentarily making direct eye contact that communicates a subtle curiosity, and for a second you think about it and then it's just gone.

Saying the Same Thing Simultaneously: Sometimes, you and your friend notice something or react to something by yelling out the same set of words. This is something that occurs rarely, but it gives you something to smile about.

Realizing You Have More Time to Sleep: Sometimes, you abruptly wake up in the middle of the night, and you think it's time to wake up, and when you look at the time, and you still have two more hours to sleep. A warm euphoric feeling shoots through your body at that moment, and then you glide back to your dreams.

The feeling after a healthy workout: There is a feeling of self-satisfaction and accomplishment that you get; this is one activity that will make you feel better and also make you look good at the same time. So when you walk out of the main door of the gym, you feel like you are on top of the world.

Relaxing Outdoors on a Sunny Day: When you are relaxing in your chair, reading your favourite book as the light breeze keeps the temperature under control, and the sun warms your skin, you feel at peace with the environment around you.

Making Someone smile: Sometimes you notice that your fellow student is under great stress due to the exams that are just coming up, so you invite them over to your place to just relax, have good food and watch a movie with a smile on their face as they enjoy yourself will make you the happiest.

Chapter 10:
5 Lessons on Being Wrong

Being wrong isn't as bad as we make it out to be. I have made many mistakes, and I have discovered five major lessons from my experiences.

1. Choices that seem poor in hindsight are an indication of growth, not self-worth or intelligence. When you look back on your choices from a year ago, you should always hope to find a few decisions that seem stupid now because that means you are growing. If you only live in the safety zone where you know you can't mess up, then you'll never unleash your true potential. If you know enough about something to make the optimal decision on the first try, then you're not challenging yourself.

2. Given that your first choice is likely to be wrong, the best thing you can do is get started. The faster you learn from being wrong, the sooner you can discover what is right. Complex situations like relationships or entrepreneurship have to <u>start before you feel ready</u> because no one can be truly ready. The best way to learn is to <u>start practicing</u>.

3. Break down topics that are too big to master into smaller tasks that can be mastered. I can't look at any business and tell you what to do. Entrepreneurship is too big of a topic. But, I can look at any website and tell you how to optimize it for building an email list because that topic is small enough for me to develop some level of expertise. If you want to get better at making accurate first choices, then play in a smaller arena. As Niels Bohr, the Nobel Prize-winning physicist, famously said, "An expert is a person who has made all the mistakes that can be made in a very narrow field."

4. The time to trust your gut is when you have the knowledge or experience to back it up. You can trust yourself to make sharp decisions in areas where you already have proven expertise. For everything else, the only way to discover what works is to adopt a philosophy of experimentation.

5. The fact that failure will happen is not an excuse for expecting to fail. There is no reason to be depressed or give up simply because you will make a few wrong choices. Even more crucial, you must try your best every time because the effort and the practice drive the learning process. They are essential, even if you fail. Realize that no single choice is destined to fail, but that occasional failure is the cost you must pay if you want to be right. Expect to win and play like it from the outset.

Your first choice is rarely the optimal choice. Make it now, stop judging yourself, and start growing.

Happy People Don't Make Excuses

"If you are interested, you'll do what's convenient. If you are committed, you'll do whatever it takes" — John Assaraff.

Read it again. Take it in. This is one of the most effective ideas I recognize in the making and proudly owning your fitness and happiness. Happy humans are dedicated to being satisfied and successful, and much less satisfied humans are normally simplest inquisitive about being satisfied.

The distinction is huge.

What it means is this. When we are truly committed to an outcome — whatever it may be: getting in shape, buying an investment property, qualifying as a vet, owning your own business — we will do whatever it takes to make it happen. There will be obstacles. With any milestone that's big or consequential, a few (or many) obstacles along the way are an inevitable part of that journey. A happy and successful person knows that and moves over or around that obstacle in whatever way they can to keep their eye focused on the outcome they want. They will try and try and try in however many ways they need to to make it happen. They are not just interested in their success, and they are incontrovertibly committed to it. They don't get thrown off at the first sign of struggle.

They are more committed to their goal than they are interested in another 45 minutes in bed or the social acceptance of joining in with a slice of cake.

When we are interested rather than committed, the main thing you will hear coming out of our mouths is excuses. "Oh, I was going to save that money, but something unexpected came up"; "I am getting back on that eating plan as soon as, but it's just been really busy at the moment" that sort of thing.

Excuses. Excuses.

This is the place where my other statement comes in, "Everything before the 'but' is BS." Smart, correct? It summarizes everything for me — everything before the "yet" is what we are keen on, instead of focusing on. On the off chance that we were submitted, there would be no "however." It would be an "and" all things being equal. For instance: "I needed to set aside that cash, something startling came up thus I needed to work three additional movements/offer some stuff to get it going" or "I'm back on that eating plan, it's been truly occupied right now thus I have needed to deny many things to get it going; however, I've done it."

www.ingramcontent.com/pod-product-compliance
Lightning Source LLC
Chambersburg PA
CBHW070923080526
44589CB00013B/1409